Forward

I've been battling disabilities all my life.

First with Charcot Marie Tooth.

Then I was diagnosed with Parkinson's Disease.

That's when my battle began.

Things have been tough

But with the support of my great family and friends

Life's a bit more bearable

I'm dedicating this book to my late Mum and Dad

Who were the loveliest people I knew

My Life

While I was growing up I knew something was wrong

I felt like I didn't belong

All my time at school I was picked on

I was glad when my school years had gone

No one understood about disabilities when I was young

But that was when my problems begun

I was first diagnosed with a muscle wasting disease

My body was never going to be at ease

I struggled to be as independent as I could

I tried to make myself understood

It's been a tough journey with a lot of ups and downs

There's not been a lot of smiles but plenty of frowns

Then 10 years ago my life was shocked again

I was diagnosed with an illness that attacks my brain

What was I going to do

Just what would I have to go through

Well the last decade has been quite a quest

And I haven't been at my best

But with my family and friends helping me

I've been able to just about cope with my disability

Fundraising

I started my fundraising 4 years ago

Would I raise any money I just didn't know

I started organising a comedy event

I couldn't believe just how good it went

Over a hundred people were there to see

4 great blokes doing the best comedy

These comedians we oh so funny

They were all gents they all donated their money

Everyone laughing was a wonderful sight

I managed to raise over a grand that first night

I couldn't stop after just doing one

That's when my fundraising really begun

I've had comedians from all over the land

I've raised over 27 grand

I'm not giving up yet I've still lots to do

And how can I fail when I've got friends like you

Narrow Minded

They sniggered when they saw me move

Why did they mock I'd nothing to prove

Things were starting to get out of hand

If only they knew and could understand

I felt sorry for them and I had a big grin

While they were pointing theirs kid chipped in

'Stop it dad, the man's disabled' they said

I could hear the cogs going round in their head

They apologised and looked rather in shame

Their kids told them they were to blame

I felt proud the kids told them off

They will think next time before they scoff

This is just what people do

They don't understand what I go through

Kids are honest at what they see

It was them that noticed the disability

Maybe their mocking will cease

When they learn about our disease

Getting up

When we wake up the first thing we dread

Is will we be able to get out of bed

With our legs being weak and very unstable

We just don't know if we will be able

We place our feet on the floor

It's got to be easy we've done it before

So we stand up and our legs start to shake

We're up legs aren't quite awake

When will they wake up nobody knows

That is the way our condition goes

We find it difficult to just get started

Be we are never downhearted

We know our illness never gives relief

We still hold onto the belief

That one day we will be pain free

And be rid of this disability

Things were easier

Long ago we could do things with ease

That was before we had this damn disease

Once we had our get up and go

Now we're so slow

Before we just got on and did it

Now we just think oh forget it

It's not like we just pack it in

It's just we find it hard to begin

We find it hard doing things now

Even though we know how

It just takes us a while

But when we do it we always smile

Although we struggle every day

We know we can do things in our own way

No need to hurry

We take our time we've no need to hurry

We do things our own way we don't worry

So what if it takes too long

We know we don't do it wrong

We don't rush we go at our own pace

W know it's not a race

We will just do things our own way

We know coming last is a small price to pay

When we get there we know we will smile

We will know our journey will be worthwhile

Same thing, different day

It's 4 in the morning and I'm wide awake

I'd love a full nights' sleep for gods' sake

I looked outside and what do I see

Only the milkman is up like me

I'd love to sleep and get a clear head

Oh I suppose I'll sleep when I'm dead

Now I'm awake I don't know what to do

I wouldn't want my wife woken up too

I've felt like I've walked for miles

I'm very tired and it's hard to find the smiles

I try to stand up but all I do is freeze

I better not move or I'll fall on my knees

Breakfast time now this should be fun

With my tremor I'll never get it done

What will I have I look all round

Whatever I have will end up on the ground

Well I'm glad that it's over that was a chore

Most of the sugar ends up on the floor

Now to get dressed this'll take ages

I'll get it done just do it in stages

Now half the days gone and I'm worn out

I've fall asleep soon of that there's no doubt

I'll just have an hour well hopefully I will

When I wake up after 3 I feel quite ill

Its tea time now what will I eat

Might be eggs they really hard to beat

Relaxing time with a sneaky drink

Only a quick pint I seem to think

Oh well after 3 more it's hard to talk

I try to go to bed but cannot walk

Oh well I best stay down here

And open another beer

You've got to laugh

My walking is a laugh when I begin

I walk like I'm a lame penguin

One leg goes left one goes right

Watching me walk is a right sight

I take 3 steps forward then 2 steps back

I never keep on the right track

It makes me laugh it's so funny

I'd give Charlie Chaplin a run for his money

I waddle like a lame duck

It must be weird if when people look

This illness thinks it brings us down

But sometimes we don't have a frown

Although we frown for a while

Sometimes we do have a smile

It's that time again

Oh well it's that time again

We are awake as usual because of the pain

It's the same as it was many times before

We see the time it says its half past four

It's ages until we can take our meds

But we know we can't stay in our beds

We will fidget and won't be able to rest

So we get up we think it's for the best

What time is this though for goodness sake

At least we are the only ones awake

That's what it does it singles us out

We know exactly what it's all about

We have to try and stay strong

We know our condition is life long

Hard to Cope

Having this condition it's hard to cope

All we can do at this time is hope

Our lives are filled with uncertainty

There's no explanation for our disability

It carries on like a wound up clock

We just have to take stock

Just what can we do

Because there's a lot we go through

What we can do is hard to say

We feel different day by day

Some days we find it hard to even smile

Some days we aren't very mobile

But sometime we feel alright

And we are up for the fight

Whatever we feel we'll never give in

We will never let this illness win

It Always Here

Another month gone the illness is still here

Can't see anything to give me a cheer

Then I look all around and what do I see

My loving family really help me

My body is slow and hard to move around

My mind's still working that's what I've found

I take my time and do things my own way

It keeps me going throughout the day

People don't understand but it's not their fault

The illness just hit me like a lightning bolt

The pain gets worse and hard to overcome

But I fight everyday at what I've become

I find the strength and you can too

You can't beat it that this is true

But don't let it win and put up a good fight

Give this illness a hell of a fright

Dreaming

When we finally sleep nothing's as it seems

Some of us have very bad dreams

I once dreamt I was eating a marshmallow

When I woke up I had no pillow

Another one I had was I slept like a log

I woke up in the fireplace next to the dog

Some wake up early with a sweat on our face

And our hearts beating a very fast pace

Our dreams can be very scary

When we go to bed it makes us very wary

We might drift into nightmare land

We don't know why or even understand

We know this disease plays with our minds

We wish we could leave it behind

I'm Still Special

I'm not an invalid I'm just a special man

I'm not a quitter I do the best I can

I'm not giving up I'm here to stay

I'm not mute I have lots to say

I'm not a faker I'm not pain free

I'm not lying I really do have a disability

I'm not saying I don't because I do

I'm not hiding just what I go through

I'm not unhappy I've just lost my smile

I'm not leaving I'm here for a while

I'm not on my own I have family and friends

I'm not into God but pray this thing will end

I'm not scared but this illness gives me a fright

I'm not defeated I'm still up for a fight

Things were easy before

The things we did that were easy before

We can't seem to do much anymore

Things like eating s hard to do

Theres many problems we have to go through

We struggle getting things done

It takes us ages once we've begun

It's hard coping with our disability

We wish we could problem free

We never moan that's not our way

Even though we struggle every single day

We crack on in silence the best we can

And get on with our own plan

We try a lot to ease the pain

We know our aches will remain

We will continue till this illness goes

Just when that will be god only knows

Getting Stressed

We start our day by trying to get dressed

This is the first time we get stressed

Simply putting on clothes is quite a quest

We manage the socks but can't do the rest

Next is our undies we give them a go

Both legs go in one hole oh no

Our t-shirt goes on inside out

What's that all about

Trying to put our shoes on is quite a sight

They get mixed up our left ones on the right

It's taken us but we are ready

When we stand up we aren't very steady

We are worn out with all we've done

That's before our days begun

This is one of the things some don't see

Things are hard with our disability

We struggle with things every single day

But we keep it quiet and don't like to say

We could make a fuss and shout out loud

But we suffer in silence because we are proud

Not looking disabled

I was in the supermarket car park

And parked in a disabled space

A woman walked up to my car

And pointed her finger in my face

'You shouldn't park there' she said

I looked and her and asked why

She stopped and took a breathe

'You're not disabled' was the reply

I thought how could she be sure

She had never seen me before

Then she just shrugged and walked off

When I got out of the door

She didn't say another word

She realised that I had a right to be there

When I opened my boot

And got into my wheelchair

What does a disabled person look like

No one knows

We don't all limp

Or wear badges on our clothes

I wasn't annoyed at this woman

I just felt sorry for her and her view

She's just like a lot of people

They haven't got a clue

Not all disabled people are the same

Some can walk alone some need a hand

All people need to do

Is to just understand

We Wish

We wish our illness would just leave

But it doesn't give us any reprieve

It's on our case both day and night

Our condition just arrived without and invite

It barged its way in and pulled up a chair

It's just not going anywhere

It settled in and started its attack

We do what we can to fight back

Although our illness is here to stay

And will be active every day

We want to be alone

Sometimes when it gets too much

We just want to be on our own

We don't want any company

We just want to be left alone

It not that we're anti social

We just need our own space

We like to have a good think

About our position in the human race

We sometimes feel so useless

Other times we feel good

These mixed feelings

Just can't be understood

We know it's this condition

That's causing us pain

It's constantly chipping at it

It just won't refrain

Tip of the Iceberg

People see the limp but what else do they see

They don't understand our disability

They don't see they anxiety we hide it well

They don't see the depression we don't tell

The pains another thing eye suffer from too

They don't see anything we go through

We lose our smell we find it hard to smile

We've suffered for quite a while

We don't like to say how we feel

Even though our illness is very real

The difficulty sleeping is also there

The restlessness and pain is hard to bare

We often find it hard to breathe

We wish this illness would leave

Sometimes we don't like to talk

Our legs are weak we can hardly walk

Our symptoms can get out of hand

So how can anyone else understand

There are many things to get our minds around

We need to keep our feet on the ground

Uncertainty

Our days are uncertain we just can't see

We don't know how we are going to be

We can't make plans which is a shame

Our condition is the one to blame

Without our illness got things done

We could have laughter and plenty of fun

But unfortunately that's not the case

We have to wait to see the smile on our face

We are either full of beans or totally bean free

That's the signs of our disability

We'd like to have some get up and go

But we just don't know

What are we going to be like we just can't say

Because we feel different that's the price we pay

All the same

We are all the same or we should be

But we have disabilities that's hard to see

We find it hard to get around

People speak to us different all around

They speak to us like we don't understand

They just carry on it can get right out of hand

It's not their fault we try to explain

We do our best so tell them again and again

We are looked at like we are second rate

I know it's very hard but we do not hate

We just laugh to hide our disgust

We find it very hard to trust

We take our time to get things done

We might be disabled but still have some fun

Treat us like adults and you will see

We are just people who have a disability

The things they say

The things some people is out of hand

It's not their fault they just don't understand

You don't look disabled is one they say

That's because they don't see us every day

Just what does a disabled person look like

It's not as if we all look alike

Some can lead a wonderful life

Some have lots of strife

Our illness affects us all as you will see

Not everyone looks like they have a disability

But one thing that is true

Is that we struggle with what we have to do

Although we are may be slower than before

We will fight to the end that's for sure

Keeping Quiet

We don't say much even though we try

We can't get it out and we know why

It's this damn illness it gets in the way

Of all the things we want to say

We have so many things going round our mind

But all the right words are hard for us to find

By the time we get our words out

No one can understand what we talk about

So we tend to keep quiet and not say anything

It takes us ages for our days to begin

No one understands this damned disease

We just hope it will cease

Depression takes hold

When depression grabs hold it's hard to shake

It plays with your mind and keeps you awake

It puts thought inside your head

Thoughts that you really do dread

Your not worth much it best if you just go

What do you do you just don't know

Will they be better off without you

The doubts are hard to go through

Although you might feel you're all alone

You are not on your own

So if you feel it's the only way

Just take a step back you only have to say

That you don't want your life to end

Talk to someone they will be your friend

Together you will find you're very strong

And those dark thoughts you had are so wrong

It Really Hurts

My pains are unbearable

My whole body aches

My backs hurting like hell

My wrists hurt with all the shakes

I can't keep my food down

My stomach's churning

My legs have got pins and needles

My hands feel like they are burning

I'm going to have a bath

And try to relax

I won't get much calm time

Because illness still attacks

It never slows down

It continues its quest

One day maybe

I might get a rest

Maybe one day

I'll just sit down and be able to be calm

Then this illness

Won't do me anymore harm

Our lives changed

Our lives have changed a hell of a lot

Think this illness has lost the plot

It's thrown so much at us we can hardly cope

All we can do now is hope

We can no longer keep up with the pace

And the smile has gone from our face

Our brain is scrambled in our head

What else will it do we just dread

He's a good player and won't show his hand

That's why it's so hard to understand

Just why he's making our lives so hard

It looks like we've been dealt the losing card

Come on show us what you've got CMT

So we can deal with our disability

So many of us

There are so many disabilities in the world

But when they are all unfurled

You're not alone you are all the same

And your illnesses are just a name

You may be slower than you were before

And you can't do things quickly anymore

But don't be sad about what you go through

Because in the end you are still you

People may do things that are out of hand

That's because they don't understand

They don't know how special you can be

Even though you have a disability

So just remember you are very strong

And you do belong

When we go out

When we go out we always have to see

If places access for our disability

We have to Google our trip before we go

Because we night not know

Will the paths be level and easy to use

If they're not we will have to refuse

Will the shops be easy to get in

We have to research before we begin

We have to plan all of our day out

So we can easily get about

I know this seems a strange way

But we have to do it if we want a good day

People don't realise the obstacles we meet

Just by going down the street

If we fall on the road we might not survive

Because unlike a cat we only have 1 life

Misunderstood

I walked into the supermarket one morning

The guard approached me without any warning

He said I seemed drunk and couldn't come in

It wasn't the way I wanted my day to begin

He made the claim without even knowing me

He didn't know I had a disability

He didn't know what to think

I'd only gone in for some milk

It was then I told him I had a disability

He looked down and apologised to me

He was embarrassed about what he'd done

But to be honest he's not the only one

Some don't understand but I don't complain

I just take a deep breath and explain

It's not their fault they aren't to blame

Not all disabled people look the same

Struggle to get going

When I wake early I struggle to get going

As soon as I stand my condition is showing

My back pain's bad my legs are wobbling

When I set off walking I'm only hobbling

I walking like I'm walking in space

Every step I do there's a grimace on my

face The pains too much I can't take much

more I ache like I've never ached before

I'll get down the stairs I know I'll get there

Then I see my target it's my comfy armchair

Finally I make it and take my seat

That was a really hazard task to complete

My legs re in so much pain

I know once I move I'll have them again

I wish this illness would have a day off

Because I can tell you all I've had enough

Unknown Troubles

Before diagnosis our lives were good

We did everything we could

Then we got the terrible news

We had an illness that gives us the blues

We didn't ask for this horrible condition

We knew we would be a lifelong mission

We had to stop and take stock

What we learned was quite a shock

We would have days with immense pain

That would happen over and over again

Our legs would be unstable and very weak

The rest of our lives looked pretty bleak

We didn't know what to do

We didn't know what we had to go through

We have to battle every day

What it would do to us we couldn't say

But we know we must stand up and fight

This illness is with us day and night

Even when we think it's the last straw

We must never call it a draw

When it started

When I started on my disability ride

My feelings were all kept inside

I didn't share what I was going through

Or just what I was going to do

I had problems when my symptoms started

It was then that they saw me downhearted

My movement got worse and I started to slow

It was then I had to let them know

When I told them I had this disease

And that my symptoms would increase

Although in my thoughts it was very dark

I was still their friend Mark

They knew it would be different for me now

They would adapt to my problem any how

On these people I knew I could depend

Because I knew they were true friends

My journey has been quite a quest

I've had ups and downs but tried my best

With friends like mine I give it my all

They have made me stand tall

They Just Don't Know

They say we won't but we will

They say we are slow but we won't stand still

They want us to stop but we still go

They have no idea just what we know

They don't understand they just don't see

They don't know how we are with our disability

They think we are weak but we are strong

They always think we are in the wrong

They want us to give up but we never will

They say they do but they don't understand

They reckon we have the upper hand

They don't know what this illness dishes out

They think they know what it's all about

They ask others how we feel

They never ask us for who it's real

They see us when we are in the blues

They wouldn't want to be in our shoes

Very much the same

Although we are all different

We are very much the same

We all struggle with our condition

And we all feel the pain

We all wish our illness would cease

And our aches would end

But we all know it won't

It's a hard illness to defend

We didn't ask for all this

We just drew the short straw

We know we won't be

Like we were before

We know it here for life

And won't go away

But we will always battle

And never call it a day

We won't give in

That's not what we do

We know we are strong enough

We need to show we're tough

Which Way

We pulled up at the junction

Which turn shall we take

If we turn left we sleep

But we turn right and are well awake

We can't control ourselves

So we just don't know

Which turn we will decide on

Or which way we will go

That's the problem we have

This illness is different every day

Our journey isn't mapped out

We don't know the way

We do what we can

We do our best

But we know it's a rocky road

And will be quite a test

But what it doesn't know

We're not as we were before

We might not win the battle

But we will win the war

Depression the monster

Depression is a monster that attacks our brain

It puts thoughts in our minds over and over again

It's hard to control no matter how much we try

It just won't let things lie

It puts dark thoughts in our head

We would love to think good things instead

But it won't let us it just chips away

We just don't know what to do or say

We try to hide it's something we don't like to show

We just pray that this monster would just go

But it's a tough enemy who won't give any reprieve

Even thought we want it to leave

It's something we just can't hide

Some of us even suggest suicide

We feel very much on our own

And want to be left alone

It's hard to deal with we get into such states

But we know it's not our turn at the Pearly gates

Other people that suffer the same understand

Just reach out you will find a helping hand

Why me?

All through my life I've been a good man

Open doors for the ladies done whatever I can

Worked all the hours for my daughter and son

Played pool with the wife but never won

Things started to change I started to slow

Things were getting worse my speech started to go

Then came the tremor and the sleepless nights

What was going on I got the right frights

My mood swings were bad, I would disagree

I didn't know what was happening to me

The Dr said I had Parkinson's it was out of the blue

I had to stop working what was I going to do

Then my symptoms began to multiply

I had to stay strong or at least try

So I keep battling and give it a fight

I may be weak but I'm up for the fight

Smile upside down

Our smiles have turned upside down

They are nothing more than just a frown

We don't mean it it's just there

All people do is point and stare

People don't understand it's not their fault

It's our illness that continues it assault

It attacked us from the very start

It makes us have a heavy heart

Although we are sad we so much want to smile

It's something we haven't done for a while

Sometimes our smile does appear

But it soon fades and will disappear

We have to carry on fighting you will see

Because of our harmful disability

Tasteless

The smell drifts in from the kitchen

Can't wait to eat this food

Then something happened

That rather changed my mood

My plate was placed in front of me

It looked rather nice

A lovely chicken curry

With some basmati rice

I pick up my folk to take a bite

It's a meal I once adored

But when I took a mouthful

It tasted like cardboard

I knew my taste buds had gone

I used to love how my food would taste

But now I just eat without the pleasure

That's a big waste

I know this is one of the symptoms

That Parkinson's like to dish out

But it's one of those things

I could right do without

We Hope

Parkinson's brings us such misery

Its symptoms are such a mystery

We hope soon to be on the mend

But this illness is so hard to defend

Our future isn't looking great

As for a cure we'll just have to wait

It's not an illness we want to shared

But it's already out there everywhere

We have no idea what our futures hold

But this illness just won't be told

It's here all the time and never stops teasing

It's looks as though it's not going to be easing

It just keeps going chipping away

It just bugs us every day

We will have the victory

And this illness will be history

No Sympathy

We don't want your ahhhs or your sympathy

We don't blame you for our disability

We might get angry but in our defence

We like to have our own independence

We used to do things a lot easier before

It's just we can do those things any more

We know exactly what to expect

We just want a little bit of respect

We will try it just might take us a bit longer

But we'll do it when we're feeling stronger

We may be weak but we all know

Whatever it is we will give it a go

Even though we aren't very fit

We will never ever quit

Unstable

We may be disabled and not very able

When I stand up my balance is very unstable

My mood changes at the drop of a hat

I can't seem to control that

But everyone who know me knows what I'm about

I'm the sort of bloke they can't do without

Because underneath my illness is a wonderful man

Who gives a lot of love whenever I can

I'm a special person as they all see

It's not my fault I have a disability

I feel down sometimes and feel very low.

But do I give in oh no

I've too much in my life yet to do

I'm going to fight my way through

We want respect

We don't want much but what we expect

Is a little bit of respect

We may be disabled and not very quick

And although our lives have become chaotic

We are still people with feelings

And know what our condition brings

Don't patronise us or feel sorry

We will fight this illness don't worry

If you don't understand don't stay silent

Speak to us we'll tell you about our ailment

If you don't ask you won't know

Why we can't plan for tomorrow

We have to just live day by day

And why sometimes we are full of dismay

Then you might realise what we go through

And what our lives have turned into

We need your help that's for sure

We all are praying for a cure

Our illness thinks we won't win

But one thing for certain is we won't give in

Ambition

Some of us use a stick some use a chair

Some walk unaided but all people do is stare

They feel sorry for us and give us sympathies

It's like it's their fault we have disabilities

There's no one to blame it just happened that way

We have to live with it day after day

We may be disabled and not as mobile

And not very often wanting to smile

But we are still human and very much alive

We still have loads of devotion and plenty of drive

We still have goals and plenty of ambition

We will not be ruled by our condition

We might not succeed but will always give it a go

One thing that won't happen is we will never say no

Look at ourselves

We look in the mirror but don't like the sight

That's what we look like after having a bad night

We've run out of matchsticks to help open our eyes

It's not a look we can easily disguise

We look so tired and feel worn out

But it's not something we complain about

It's just one of many things we battle with each day

We don't let our problems get in our way

Although we get frustrated from time to time

We know with our condition it's a big mountain to climb

But we are fighters so we begin

Because we're strong and will never give in

Seconds Out

We put on our gloves and enter the ring

We have no idea what our opponent will bring

The bell rings and the fight begins

No one knows which of us wins

It comes out jabbing causing us pain

Our defence seems to be in vain

It continues the attack into round two

Just what other things is it going to do

The fight goes on though rounds 3 and 4

But we are are still standing we don't hit the floor

Rounds 5, 6, 7 are just like the rest

This fight is becoming a very hard test

It keeps on punching but we are still fine

Are defence is here at the end of round nine

Final round starts ding ding goes the bell

This is when we start to do well

We come out fighting with all our might

Because we are well up for this fight

We might not win but we will stay strong

If we do we will never do wrong

Heating's always on

Well it's getting colder so the t-shirt is gone

It may be cold but the heating's not going on

They tell me they're cold when they come down

So I tell them they have a dressing gown

They also have gloves scarves and a hat

It's staying off so that's that

Who am I kidding this is a fight I won't win

So now my sweating is going to begin

So while I'm sat here I'm not like the rest

While they are all wrapped up I'm in shorts and a vest

'I'm turning it off soon' I warn her

'It's like sitting in a bloody sauna'

But my speech falls on deaf ears

Just like it's been for the last 13 years

I'll just have to put up with the heat

She's an opponent I'll never beat

Even my grandson is on my case

How can I say no with the look on his face

Legs wearing out

My legs are wearing out walking has becoming a test

When I start moving one goes east one goes west

I never seem to stay on the right track

When I take 3 steps forward I always do 2 steps back

It's a right battle to go walk anywhere

When I go outside I have to beware

I so unstable I'm liable to trip

Or step too far forward I tend to slip

When I do fall there's only one place I go

And that's arse over elbow

I have to walk careful just to make sure

That I don't end up sprawled on the floor

It's my conditions that causes my woes

I put up with it because that's how it goes

Take our time

All we get from people is a lot of sympathy

We would rather they see us than our disability

We are still people with so much to give

We aren't dead yet we so want to live

When things are done its at our own pace

We would rather compete than win the race

It's a bit like the tortoise and the hare

We take our time but we will always get there

The morale of this poem is you don't have to be fast

Just do your best and you won't come last

So no matter what this illness throws at you

Only you know what you go through

All you need to do is do your best

And you might just be seen as equal to the rest

Strictly Taboo

Talking about sex and disability is strictly taboo

It's a subject we don't like to do

It's not something that likes to be discussed

With our condition sex isn't a must

It's not on the agenda like it may have been before

It's just something that's not important any more

It's not an issue in our lives at all

In fact it's an issue we see as small

We find were too tired to do the deed

Even if we do feel the need

But when it doesn't happen it's ok

We'll just try again another day

Some of us don't try for a good while

Because some of us can't even raise a smile

Sing the winning song

The flowers will bloom the sun will shine

I think this year will be our time

If we set ourselves goals we will no doubt succeed

If we give it our all we will indeed

No more negative thoughts about this disease

Even if our symptoms may increase

We must look beyond the clouds to see the sun

Then we will feel we have temporarily won

If we battle together day by day

We can help to keep our condition at bay

So join me my friends together we are strong

One day we will be singing the winning song

Tormenting Us

But then Mr P has his way

If we sleep well we feel ready for the day

He turns our tremors on to fast

God knows how long it will last

It's not long before he's at it again

He hits us with the pain

We try our best to stay tough

Because after all he's done we've had enough

Let's hope he stops with his playing

Then we might finish swaying

Come on Mr P give us a chance

We have to be strong enough to take a stance

But he has so much more in store

He gives us a lot more

But what he doesn't seem to know

Is that we are a worthy foe

So come on Mr P give us your best

Because together we are up to the test

What's our illness

People see the tremors what else do they see

They don't see things about our disability

The pains another thing eye suffer from too

They don't see anything we go through

We lose our smell we find it hard to smile

We suffered with symptoms for quite a while

We don't like to say how we feel

Even though our illness is very real

The difficulty sleeping is also there

The restlessness and sciatica is hard to bare

We often find it hard to breathe

We wish this illness would just leave

Our speech is bad we find it hard to talk

Our legs are weak we can hardly walk

Our symptoms can get out of hand

So how can anyone else understand

Hard to Shake

Whose depression is it? We all know

We are very sad though

It really is a tale of woe

All we can do is frown. We cry hello

We try to give our depression a shake

The crying keeps us awake

The only other sound is the rain

It send bad thoughts to our brain

The depression is cold, fierce and deep

All we want to do is sleep

Until then we continue to cry

All we can do is try

The dark thoughts we very much dread

With thoughts of sadness in his head

Our thoughts we cannot hide

Some of us consider suicide

We try to fight as best we can

But depression has done its worse since it began

No relief

Having illness gives us no relief

Illnesses are chronic beyond belief

We can't forget the prolonged pain

They affect our lives over and over again

Will there ever be a cure

We can never be for sure

Disorder is, in its way, the mental signs of condition

Above all others is the affection

They play with our lives every day

We just hope our illness goes away

Grandson's here

Daybreak's here and there's not a sound

Nobody seems to be around

Then as I let the dogs out I hear a noise

Its my grandson playing with his toys

When he sees me he has a massive grin

What a great way for my day to begin

He's full of energy at any time day or night

To see him smiling is a wonderful sight

He gives me something no medicine can do

The love in his heart that always shines through

So listen here my illnesses I know you're there

With my grandson by my side you haven't got a prayer

Join us

We don't want much but what we do expect

Is a little bit of respect

We may be disabled and not very quick

And although our lives have become chaotic

We are still people with feelings

And know what our condition brings

Don't patronise us or feel sorry

We will fight this illness don't worry

If you don't understand don't stay silent

Speak to us we will tell you about our ailment

If you don't ask you won't know

Why we can't plan for tomorrow

We have to just live day by day

And why sometimes we are full of dismay

Then you might realise what we go through

And what our lives have turned into

We need your help that's for sure

We all are praying for a cure

Our illness thinks we won't win

One thing's for certain we won't give in

Stand strong

Other people get on with their lives we see

But it's hard for us to do with our disability

Our lives change every day

We can't seem to keep this illness at bay

Other can make future plans

We don't know if we can

Their lives might run the same direction

But ours will deviate because of our condition

We would like it if we drove the same road

The roads are bad due to our heavy load

We may have a different wheel

But we know how we feel

Our pains are with us forever

If we stay strong and stand together

We might never beat this thing

But one thing we'll never do is give in

We give it our all

No one knows how our illness affects us all

We have to concentrate when we walk in case we fall

Others take it for granted we wish we could

But it takes us long enough to just remain stood

Then the pain strikes with every step we take

When we've finished our legs and backs ache

We do try to disguise the pains we feel

But very hard for us to conceal

The pain's constant it doesn't cease

The aching doesn't decrease

But although we aren't very stable

We do what we are able

Whatever this condition has sent

We give it 110%

We should give in by how we are treated

But we will never be defeated

My Parkinson's Ride

When I started on my Parkinson's ride

My feelings were all kept inside

I didn't share what I was going through

Or just what I was going to do

People saw my problem when my tremor started

It was then that they saw me get downhearted

My movement got worse and I started to slow

It was then I had to let them know

When I told them I had this disease

And that my symptoms would increase

Although in my thought it was very dark

It didn't bother them I was still their friend Mark

They knew things would be different for me

now They would just adapt to my problem any

how On these people I knew I could depend

Because I knew they were true friends

My journey has been quite a quest

I've had ups and downs but tried my best

With friends like mine encouraging me to give it my all

They have made me stand tall

Waiting for sunshine

The sky is clear the sun is blazing

The sights that we're seeing are quite amazing

This is my dream but for now it's not true

It's a nightmare the things we go through

Some of us shake some have lots of pain

We do have the same degeneration of the brain

The symptoms are getting worse day by day

Some of us are in a really bad way

We dream of being perfect and be rid of this disease

Then we can rest and feel at ease

We don't ask for much just a little relief

But all Parkinson does is give us grief

This book

This book is all about the struggles we go though

And the things we have to do

Being disabled we find it hard to cope

Although what we do have is hope

That one day there will be a cure

When that will be we can't be sure

There's so much research been done

It's been a long time since these have begun

Will we be the ones who will be free

And be finally be rid of our disability

We keep everything crossed fingers and toes

When will we get the cure no one knows

My Rock

She's my rock always there for me

She helps me cope with my disability

She'll do anything for me thats for sure

She may even love me more than before

Our relationship changed a hell of a lot

But that does bother her one jot

She understands what I go through

Nothing's too much for her to do

I try my best to show her how I feel

My love for her is oh so real

We've been together now for 14 years

There have been both smiles and tears

Sometimes we don't get along

But our love for each is very strong

Tough Journey

Our journeys seem to go on for miles

And there have not been many smiles

We have been on this road for many years

It has brought us so many tears

We don't know where this road will go

There is no maps that will let us know

All we know is there will be a lot of dead ends

But we will be on our trek with all our friends

We meet these friends on our way

They join us every single day

Although it will be quite an adventure

We are ready for this venture

There will be obstacles ahead of us in our quest

But we won't give in we will do our very best

Where we will end we'll have to wait and see

To see if we can conquer this disability

So Hard To Understand

When people see us struggle to stand

Why don't people understand

It's hard to explain just how we feel

We can't tell them although it's quite real

When we try to do things real slow

They take over and just go

They want everything done at their pace

We can't hurry it's not a race

They tut and walk off when we lag behind

If they could just get it in their mind

Although we are slow and will never win.

We will never ever give in

So stay with us from the start

And we will show we have the heart

Very much the same

Our symptoms vary but we are all the same

Our illnesses are only different in name

We all suffer in different ways

But we feel the same on different days

The pains always there from morning to night

We may not win but we're up for a fight

It's a fight like none before

We may win the battle but we won't win the war

The fight has been life long

We must try to stay strong

Our condition doesn't look like fading

It just continues with its body invading

Our minds get scrambled just like eggs

It affects us from our heads down to our legs

We just don't know how we are going to be

That's what it's like having a disability

Mixed Up Minds

Our mind is cloudy in our head

It's the outcome that we dread

Some stay solid but others aren't as strong

Some let these thoughts prolong

The truth is depression is a scary threat

There no answer to it quite yet

Some take the easy way out

But there's a doubt

If you're feeling full of despair

Reach out there's someone out there

They will comfort you and lend an ear

Then maybe your depression will disappear

Playing Tricks

My illness constantly plays tricks on me

It laughs at my disability

It plays with me like I'm a toy

I try but can't see any joy

It has me thinking I'm a fit man

I try to do the best I can

It also put dark thoughts deep in my mind

It's not being very kind

It just likes to lark around doing his worse

That's why I put my words in verse

I won't win this battle against this heartless foe

He's going to fill my life with woe

Its attack is hard to defend

I'd rather have him a friend

My Great Family

My family were shocked about my disability

What would they do how would they treat me

Some turned their back and turned up their nose

I suppose that's the way it goes

My Mrs and my kids weren't bothered one bit

They were the ones that helped me deal with it

I have bad times but there are still there

They weren't going anywhere

They help me with my daily tasks

They help me with anything I ask

Nothing is too much trouble they will lend a hand

Because they really do understand

My grandson Charlie is a wonderful young lad

Seeing him makes me so glad

He knows just what I need to do

He runs around and helps me he's only 2

I'm lucky to have a great family by my side

They make things steady on my bumpy ride

Hostage

The snow is like a blanket upon the ground

It sparkles like crystals all around

It covers as far as we can see

It won't be here long unlike our disability

That will be with us forever and a day

It's the price we all have to pay

We wish our condition would give us a break

It's a bitter pill to take

It wouldn't be so bad if it want for the pain

There's all sorts of things going in our brain

We can't leave these thoughts behind

We are being held Hostage To The Mind

Printed in Great Britain
by Amazon